The Old Staircase

By Linda Shefcik

Illlustrated by Erin Eitter Kono

Holly, Simon, and Laura wandered deeper into the enormous forest in search of autumn foliage. Holly's science project was to collect various types of leaves.

"I only need one more leaf to defeat Sandy Curtis!" Holly exclaimed.

"What kind of tree are we looking for?" Simon asked.

"A dogwood," Holly replied.

"Wait!" Laura exclaimed. "I found it!"

"How do you know?" Simon asked.

"Because I just heard it barking," Laura laughed.

"Funny—not," Holly answered.

Suddenly, the wind howled. Yellow, orange, and red leaves showered the weathered dirt trail, and darkness overtook the sky.

"We shouldn't stay," Laura said. "This is dangerous. Let's go."

"The weather report said it wouldn't rain until tonight," said a confused Holly, as thunder crashed and lightning illuminated the mysterious sky.

"The weather report was incorrect. I'm getting out of this nightmare," Simon shouted. He turned and bolted down the trail.

"Wait! Where are you going? It's obvious that we need to go in the opposite direction," Laura shouted.

Dark clouds quickly plunged the adventurers into darkness. The deep rumble of thunder sounded like a monster's growl. Holly, Laura, and Simon quickly navigated their way down a twisted wilderness trail, but the storm followed them at a ferocious speed.

The trail soon brought them to a spacious field. In the distance was an abandoned old house. The trees and bushes surrounding the strange-looking house seemed as if they were slowly swallowing it.

"Let's enter that house for protection!" Simon yelled.

"Protection? It looks too spooky to be safe!" Laura shouted.

But huge raindrops and loud booms of thunder convinced Laura that maybe it wasn't a bad idea.

The house leaned to the right and looked like it could be destroyed with one push. The upstairs windows were shattered. As the friends jumped onto the porch, the house creaked. At that moment the front door mysteriously blew open.

Debris littered the floor of the living room; the chalky walls were splattered with old paint.

"Just think," Holly said, inspecting the structure. "Some family probably lived here."

"I can't understand why they left this beautiful home," Simon said.

"Is it just my imagination, or is there a pair of eyes peering at me?" Laura said, pointing at the corner of the room.

There sat a doll trapped by spider webs.

Just as Holly was about to pick up the doll, a
crash thundered upstairs. Holly jumped, and Laura
screamed. Simon yelled, "I'm leaving now!"

"Simon, get back here! We're in this together,"
whispered Holly. "Hello!" Holly yelled up the
staircase. "Is anyone up here?"

They heard a clapping noise from upstairs.

"Simon," whispered Laura. "See who's up
there."

"Only if you accompany me. I'm not going
alone," Simon answered.

"We'll all go," Holly said. Simon and Laura
slowly and unhappily followed Holly up the stairs.

Slowly the expedition approached the second floor to investigate the intriguing clapping noise. Holly reached out and slowly pushed the creaking door open.

Caw! Caw! A huge raven sound as it darted toward them.

Holly screamed, and Laura and Simon jumped. The rattled raven dashed out the window.

"Look!" Holly yelled, pointing out the window. "That tree! It's a dogwood!"

The rain slowed to a drizzle. The three friends headed home, comparing notes on the great dogwood adventure.